CONTENTS

THE EARTH'S BEGINNING

No one really understands how the **Universe** came to be. Most scientists believe it all started around **14,000 million years ago**, with a giant explosion called the **Big Bang**.

The **Big Bang** created a giant fireball, which cooled and expanded, forming tiny particles called **matter**.

As the particles spread out, the Universe began to grow, and thick clouds of hydrogen and helium gases formed. Over time, these clouds joined together to make dense clusters, which eventually formed the first galaxies.

Some 10,000 million years after the Big Bang, our **Sun** and the **planets** of our **Solar System** formed in a **spiral galaxy** called the **Milky Way.**

Fun Facts

From 1930 Pluto was believed to be the ninth planet of our Solar System. In 2006, Pluto was removed from the list for being too small. It is now called a dwarf planet or a Kuiper Belt Object.

Each planet has a fixed path around the Sun.

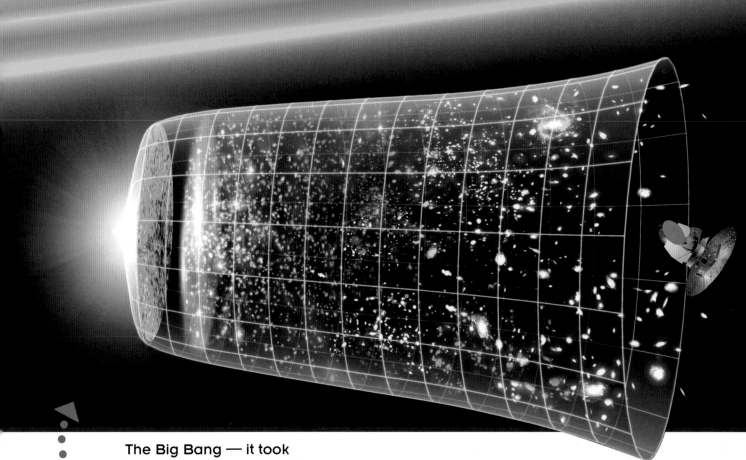

The Big Bang — it took less than a second and the universe was formed.

The **Earth orbits the Sun** at a distance of **149.6 million kilometres**, which makes it just the right temperature for **water** to exist as a **liquid**, as well as in solid form (**ice**), and as a **vapour**.

The Earth also has a **breathable atmosphere**, which, when viewed from space, looks like a very thin blue layer surrounding our planet.

These characteristics mean that the Earth, unlike any of the other planets in our Solar System, is able to **support life**.

- The name "Earth" is at least 1,000 years old. All the other planets are named after Greek & Roman Goddesses. "Earth" is an English/German word which simply means "ground".

- Though the planet is called Earth, only about thirty per cent of its surface is actually 'earth'. The rest is water!

Did You Know ?

In one second, the Earth travels about 30 km (19 miles) around the Sun.

THE EARLY EARTH

We can only see a tiny corner of the Universe from Earth, and have only been able to explore a miniscule fraction of it.

There is no real proof about how the Universe came to be, or how the Earth was formed, but most of the information scientists have gathered about the Earth's past comes from **rocks**.

Most rocks are formed layer by layer over many thousands, or even millions of years. By examining the different layers, **geologists** can make observations about what conditions were like on Earth throughout various stages of its history.

Two thirds of the Earth's surface is covered in **water**. Scientists believe that the oceans were home to the Earth's very **first life forms**.

Fossils like this one of the Cambrian period prove that life existed on Earth millions and millions of years ago.

Fun Facts

Throughout the Devonian Period (415-355 million years ago) the climate was hot and dry and water levels fell. One group of fish adapted so that they could breathe both in and out of the water. These were the earliest amphibians.

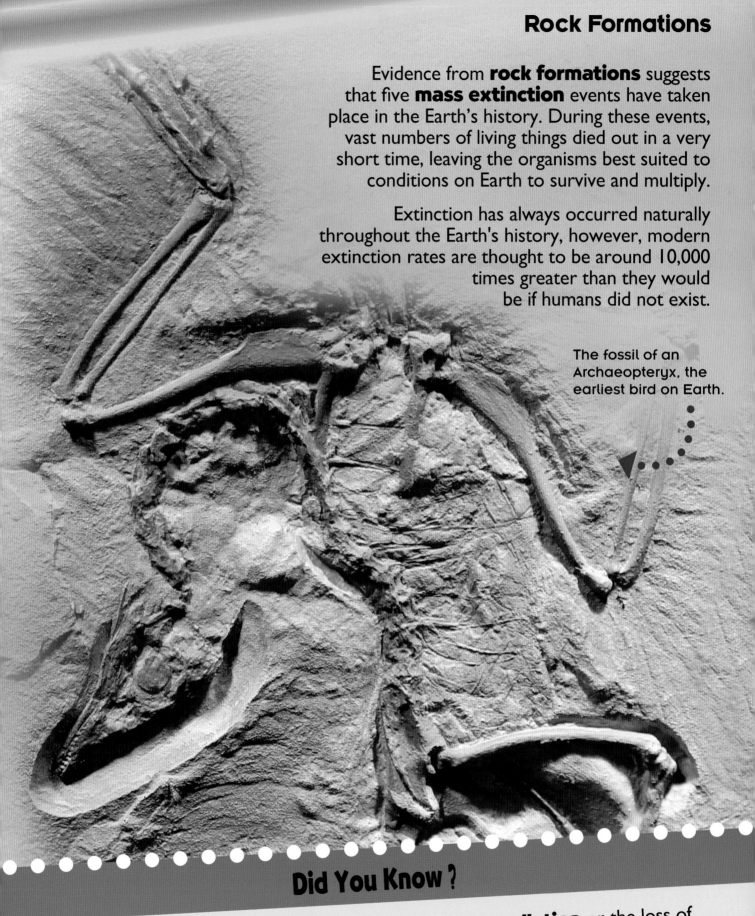

Rock Formations

Evidence from **rock formations** suggests that five **mass extinction** events have taken place in the Earth's history. During these events, vast numbers of living things died out in a very short time, leaving the organisms best suited to conditions on Earth to survive and multiply.

Extinction has always occurred naturally throughout the Earth's history, however, modern extinction rates are thought to be around 10,000 times greater than they would be if humans did not exist.

The fossil of an Archaeopteryx, the earliest bird on Earth.

Did You Know ?

Modern extinction events are almost always caused by **pollution** or the loss of **habitats** - direct results of the growing human population's increasing demands on the Earth's dwindling natural resources.

THE STRUCTURE OF THE EARTH

The Earth is made up of different layers, which formed when the planet was young, and extremely hot.

These layers are all held in place by the enormous force of **gravity** acting upon the planet's **inner core**, an incredibly hot ball of **iron** and **nickel**.

Some of the layers are partly **molten**, which means that they contain extremely hot liquid, and are covered by an outer layer of **solid rock,** called the **crust**.

The rock that makes up the surface of the Earth is constantly changing as more and more layers are added. Its composition can be divided into three different types of rock:

The mantle that lies below the crust constitutes almost two-thirds of the Earth's mass.

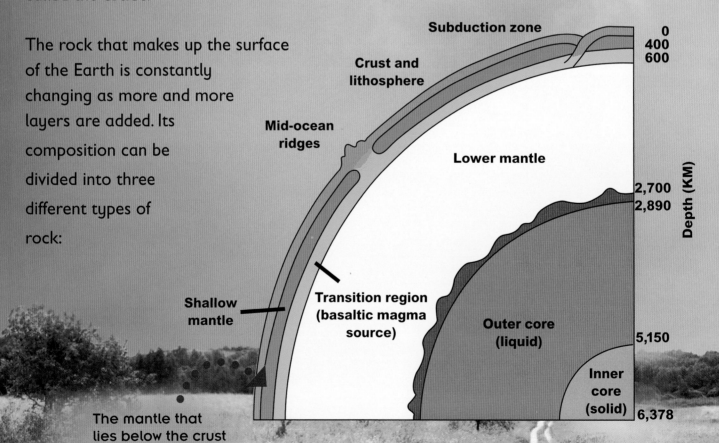

Subduction zone

Crust and lithosphere

Mid-ocean ridges

Lower mantle

Shallow mantle

Transition region (basaltic magma source)

Outer core (liquid)

Inner core (solid)

Depth (KM)

0
400
600
2,700
2,890
5,150
6,378

Fun Facts

The Earth's inner core is so hot that it could melt metal! It remains solid because it is surrounded by such immense pressure.

Igneous rock is formed when **molten** rock cools and becomes solid.

Sedimentary rock is formed when **sediments** (such as rock particles) are deposited by water, buried, and squashed into layers called **strata**.

Metamorphic rock is formed when existing rock is changed from its original form by intense **heat** or **pressure**.

The Earth's crust is thickest below the continents.

Crust: **Temperature**: Around 22°C. **State**: Solid. **Composition**: Oceanic crust made up of iron, oxygen, silicon, magnesium, and aluminium. Continental crust is made up of granite, sedimentary rocks, and metamorphic rocks.

Upper Mantle: **Temperature**: 1,400°C – 3,000°C. **State**: Solid and melted (liquid) rock. **Composition**: Iron, oxygen, silicon, magnesium, and aluminium

Lower Mantle: **Temperature**: 3,000°C. **State**: Solid. **Composition**: Iron, oxygen, silicon, magnesium, and aluminium.

Inner Core: **Temperature**: 4,000°C – 6,000°C. **State**: Liquid. **Composition**: Iron, nickel, sulphur, and oxygen.

Outer Core: **Temperature**: 5,000°C - 6,000°C. **State**: Solid. **Composition**: Iron and nickel.

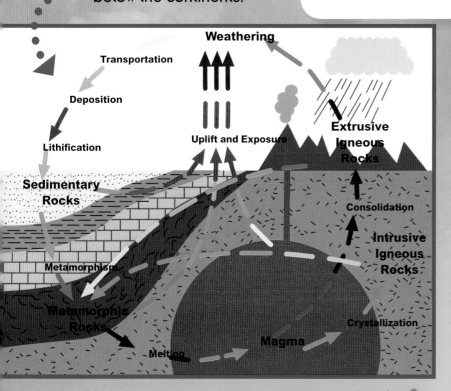

The structural secrets buried deep inside the Earth are revealed through the study of **seismic waves**, which are caused by earthquakes, explosions, and the movements of our oceans.

There are two different types of seismic wave: **shear waves**, which cannot travel through liquids, and **pressure waves**, which are able to move through both liquids and solids. These waves show that the Earth is made up of five different layers, all of varying thicknesses or **densities**.

Did You Know?

Estimates of the temperature of the Earth's inner core vary, but scientists believe it is probably between 5,000 - 7,000°C (9,000 - 13,000°F).

ROCKS, MINERALS, & CRYSTALS

The rock that makes up the surface of the Earth is constantly changing. Over ground it is affected by **weather conditions** and **water**, while beneath it is melted by heat from the Earth's **mantle** and squeezed by **high pressures** from deep within our planet.

All rocks can be categorized into three groups - **sedimentary, igneous**, and **metamorphic** - according to how they were formed, and what changes they have undergone.

Rock changes can be caused by forces such as **heat**, **pressure**, and **erosion**. This continual process of change, and the breaking down of rock into new forms, is known as the **rock cycle**.

There are all sorts of rocks, minerals, and crystals buried in your excavation kit. Below are some of the specimens you might find. Can you match the pictures with your discoveries to name what you've found?

Pumice is a volcanic rock produced when lava escapes from a volcano.

Sandstone is a medium grained, common rock mostly made up of quartz.

Calcite is a calcium carbonate mineral commonly used in cements and mortars.

Chalcopyrite is often referred to as "yellow copper" because of its colour and high copper content.

Tiger Eye is so named because it is thought to resemble the eye of a tiger. It was worn by Roman soldiers who believed it would protect them in battle.

Sericite is a fine-grained mineral with a silky sheen.

Green Aventurine is a form of quartz that is thought to bring good luck.

Desert Rose is the name given to crystal clusters of gypsum or barite. They are full of sand grains and are thought to resemble rose flowers.

Yellow Jade is just one of the colours of jade gemstones; they also occur in green, white, orange, yellow, lavender, grey, and black.

Amethyst is a violet variety of quartz. Its name comes from the Ancient Greek phrase for "not intoxicated" because it was believed to protect its owner from drunkenness!

Rose Quartz is distinguishable by its pink colour and has been a recognized symbol of love and beauty since ancient times.

Fluorite is well known for its rich variety of colours, ranging from purple, blue, green, and yellow to pink, black, red, and orange.

Sodalite is a blue mineral first discovered in Greenland.

Granite is a very hard stone that contains large quartz crystals.

Rhondonite a pink metamorphic rock with black manganese oxide veins running through it.

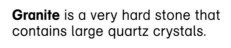

Jceland Spar is a transparent variety of calcium carbonate first discovered in Iceland.

Agate is known for its concentric patterns and is made up of many tiny crystals that can only be viewed under a microscope.

Basalt is formed when lava from a volcano cools quickly on the Earth's surface.

Obsidian is a naturally occurring volcanic glass produced when lava erupts from a volcano and cools rapidly with minimum crystal growth.

Red Jasper is an opaque, fine-grained variety of Chalcedony. Jasper is found in a variety of colours.

Malachite is a carbonate crystal with dark and light green banded areas.

Tourmaline is sometimes referred to as the "Rainbow Gemstone" because it occurs in such a wide variety of colours, though black is the most common.

Pyrite, also known as "Fools Gold" looks a lot like gold, but is, in fact, a mineral composed of iron sulfide.

Blue Aragonite is a carbonate mineral, and a component of many natural substances such as pearl and coral.

THE SURFACE OF THE EARTH

The thickness of the Earth's crust varies from between **5 kilometres** and **70 kilometres**. Thicker, **continental crust** forms the land, and thinner, **oceanic crust** makes up the ocean floors.

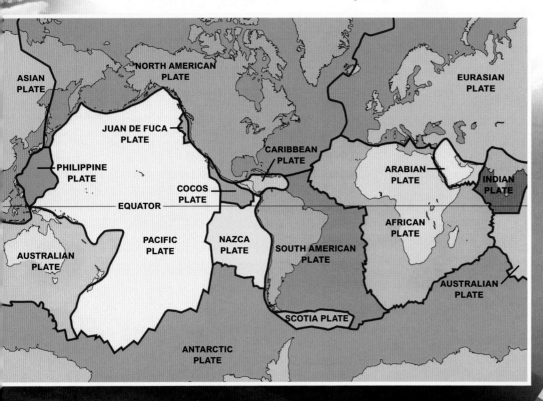

ASIAN PLATE

NORTH AMERICAN PLATE

EURASIAN PLATE

JUAN DE FUCA PLATE

CARIBBEAN PLATE

ARABIAN PLATE

PHILIPPINE PLATE

COCOS PLATE

INDIAN PLATE

EQUATOR

AFRICAN PLATE

PACIFIC PLATE

NAZCA PLATE

SOUTH AMERICAN PLATE

AUSTRALIAN PLATE

AUSTRALIAN PLATE

SCOTIA PLATE

ANTARCTIC PLATE

The Crust

The crust is broken into irregular **plates**, which drift over the **upper mantle** layer near the Earth's surface.

Always on the Move

We use the word **"tectonics"** to describe the movement of these plates: some slide past one another, while others come together, and still others drift apart.

Because all the Earth's plates fit together like a giant jigsaw puzzle, the movement of one plate affects the others all around it.

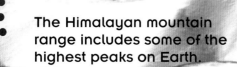
The Himalayan mountain range includes some of the highest peaks on Earth.

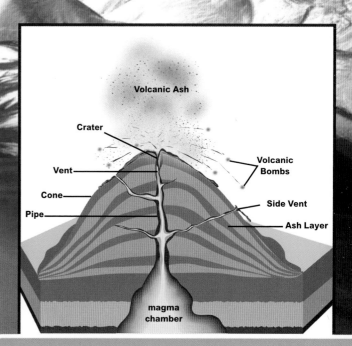

Volcanic Ash

Crater

Vent

Cone

Pipe

Volcanic Bombs

Side Vent

Ash Layer

magma chamber

Fascinating Features

Many of the Earth's most fascinating features occur at **plate boundaries**, where different plates meet. **Mountain ranges**, for example, are formed when two **continental plates collide**.

Volcanoes, ocean trenches, and **earthquakes** are all the result of the movement of the Earth's plates.

- The movement of the liquid outer core is believed to create the Earth's magnetic field. This field creates two poles called magnetic North and Magnetic South.

- Around 250 million years ago there was just one massive landmass called Pangaea.

Did You Know ?

225 million years ago, Pangaea started to divide, and the continents we know today began to form.

MOUNTAINS

When plates on the ocean floor move apart, **magma** from the Earth's **mantle** wells up along the boundary. Over time, the magma cools and hardens, forming a **mountain range** or **ridge** of new crust.

Spreading ridges occur as the movement continues, and more magma wells up along the centre of the existing ridge.

A boundary where a new crust is formed is called a **constructive boundary**.

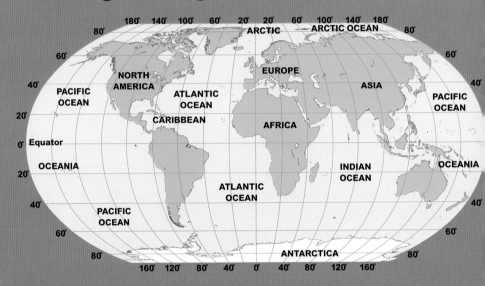

Destructive boundaries, or **subduction zones**, occur where one plate is forced beneath another, and begins to melt.

Sometimes, two plates push together above the ground, causing the Earth's crust to buckle and fold upwards. These movements form high mountain ranges called **fold mountains**.

It is near impossible to live in freezing Antarctica.

ount Everest, in the Himalayas, is the llest mountain on Earth above sea level.

you measure the height of mountains from e centre of the Earth, however, Everest ouldn't even get into the highest 20!

his is because the Earth isn't a perfect phere - it is slightly squashed, and bulges ut in the middle, giving an advantage to ountains situated along the equator.

Fun Facts

The oldest person ever to climb Everest is Yuichiro Miura of Japan, who was 80 years old at the time of his climb!

- The world's highest unclimbed mountain is Gangkhar Puensum in Bhutan, which is the 40th highest mountain in the world.

- Due to the tectonic plate movement, Everest grows about 4mm every year.

Did You Know ?

Chimborazo, in Ecuador, is actually the highest mountain in the world, and the closest to space, when measured from the centre of the Earth, because of the planet's strange shape!

17

EARTHQUAKES

The strain caused by the movement of the Earth's plates sometimes causes cracks, or **faults**.

These faults often occur at weak areas, which will be prone to more movement or cracking. All **plate boundaries** are **major faults** in the Earth's surface, and would have begun as minor cracks.

The constant movement of plates across the Earth's **mantle** causes pressure to build at faults, as well as at the plate boundaries themselves.

Earthquakes occur when a sudden slippage of rock causes the pressure within a fault to be released quickly.

Most are too weak to be felt, but some are highly destructive, and leave utter devastation in their wake.

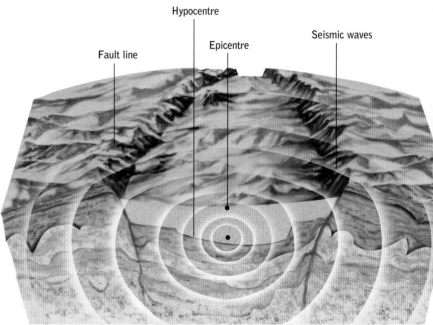

Hypocentre

Fault line

Epicentre

Seismic waves

The point at which an earthquake starts is called the **focus**, and is usually between 5 and 15 kilometres underground. The point on the surface directly above the focus is called the **epicentre**. **Seismic waves** travel from the focus in all directions.

Interesting Facts

In 1556 an earthquake in China killed 830,000 people.

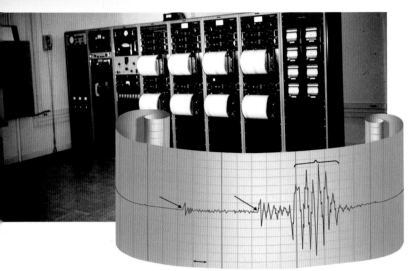

▼ The instruments at Honolulu geophysical observatory monitor tidal levels at remote sites throughout the Pacific Basin. These are used to warn about tsunamis.

Seismologists

Seismologists are scientists who study earthquakes. They are able to predict the occurrence of major earthquakes by observing plate movements using laser beams.

- According to old African folk tales, Earthquakes are caused by wives calling the names of their mother-in-laws!

- According to recent research, rats flee an area before an earthquake hits.

- According to Japanese mythology, a giant cat fish called Namazu is responsible for all earthquakes!

Changes in behaviour

Sometimes, changes in animal behavior have alerted people to the likelihood of an earthquake. 96% of male toads in a population abandoned their breeding site just days before an earthquake struck L'Aquila in Italy, probably because they detected the release of gases and charged particles in the lead up to the quake. Similarly, snakes came out of hibernation early in the day before a 1975 earthquake in China, disturbed by the early vibrations in the ground.

The San Andreas Fault in California is the point where the Pacific Plate and the North American Plate move against each other.

Did You Know?

The biggest earthquake ever felt in Britain was in 1580. It caused a tsunami that sunk 150 ships and drowned 120 people in Dover.

VOLCANOES

Volcanoes form when two plates pull apart, and **magma** within the Earth's **mantle** rises to the surface, bursting out in a violent explosion called an **eruption**.

At this stage, the **magma** becomes known as **lava**.

Most volcanoes form along **plate boundaries**, or under the sea, where the Earth's crust is thinnest, but some form in the middle of plates, at **hot spots**.

Most volcanoes erupt with enormous force, throwing lava, fireballs, and ash high into the air.

Ash and smoke

Central vent

Magma

Conduit

Chamber

Supervolcanoes

Supervolcanoes occur when **magma** in the Earth's **mantle** rises to the **crust** but is unable to break through. Over time, **pressure builds** in a large (and growing) **magma pool**, eventually bursting out in a devastating explosion. Such explosions are rare: it is thought that the last supervolcano eruption took place in **Sumatra** some 74,000 years ago.

The volcanic materials gradually pile up around the vent, forming a volcanic mountain, or volcano.

Hot Spots

Scientists believe that hot spots form when **currents of magma** burn through the Earth's crust and burst out of the surface. These particularly hot currents are called **plumes.**

Major hot spots include the Iceland hot spot, the Reunion hot spot, and the Afar hot spot, located beneath northeastern Ethiopia.

Volcanic eruptions throw up three kinds of materials: lava, rocks, and gases.

- One in 20 people in the world live within "danger range" of an active volcano.

- Volcanoes don't only occur on land - they form under the sea, and beneath ice caps too!

- Lava can reach temperatures of up to 1,250°C.

Subduction Zones

Volcanoes can also form at **subduction zones**, where one plate is forced beneath another, and begins to melt.

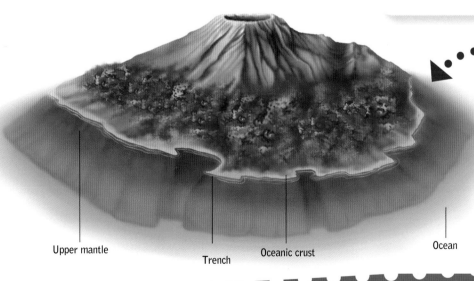

Volcanic eruptions in the ocean deposit large amounts of lava on the ocean floor. Over time, this builds above sea level, forming an island.

Upper mantle

Trench

Oceanic crust

Ocean

Did You Know ?

The word "volcano" comes from the name "Vulcan", the Roman God of Fire.

THE EARTH'S ATMOSPHERE

Our planet is surrounded by a blanket of gases called the **atmosphere**, which is held in place by **gravity**, and makes it possible for living things to survive on Earth.

Viewed from space, the atmosphere looks like a thin blue haze, because of the way in which sunlight is filtered through the **atmospheric gases**.

It is these gases that enable living things to **breathe** the air around them. They also act as a shield, protecting us from the Sun's harmful **ultraviolet rays**.

The early atmosphere would have been **poisonous** to living things.

A breathable atmosphere only began to form when the first **plant-like organisms** appeared in the Earth's oceans. They used **light** from the **Sun** to make food from **water** and **carbon-dioxide**, releasing **oxygen** into the air as a by-product.

Millions of years later, enough oxygen had collected in the Earth's atmosphere to support new, more complex life forms.

Burning **fuels** and **forests** has released lots of extra **carbon dioxide** into the atmosphere, which has built up over time, trapping the Sun's heat around the Earth. This is known as the **greenhouse effect,** and is likely to cause **global warming**.

Fun Facts

If you went soaring through the atmosphere in a hot air balloon, you would find it harder to breathe the higher you went as the atmosphere got thinner!

Troposphere: The troposphere begins at the surface of the Earth and extends upwards by around 8 to 14.5 kilometres (5 to 9 miles). This part of the atmosphere is the most dense. Almost all weather occurs in this region.

Stratosphere: This layer begins just above the troposphere and extends for a further 50 kilometers (31 miles). The ozone layer, which absorbs and scatters ultraviolet radiation from the Sun, is in this layer.

Mesosphere: Meteors burn up in the mesosphere, which starts just above the stratosphere and extends up to 85 kilometers (53 miles) high.

Thermosphere: Aurora and satellites occur in the thermosphere layer, which begins just above the mesosphere and extends 600 kilometers (372 miles).

Ionosphere: The ionosphere grows and shrinks according to solar conditions and can be divided into further sub-regions. It contains a high concentration of electrons and ionized atoms, and is able to reflect radio waves. This region is what makes radio communications possible.

Exosphere: This is the outermost limit of the Earth's atmosphere. It extends from the top of the thermosphere to around 10,000 km (6,200 mi) high.

Layered like an Onion!

600 km (372 miles)

Thermosphere

85 km (53 miles)

Mesosphere

50 km (31 miles)

Stratosphere

12 km (7.5 miles)

Troposphere

The troposphere is where you find life on Earth.

Did You Know?

The mixture of gases in the atmosphere has taken over 4.5 billion years to evolve! Around 99% of the atmosphere is made up of oxygen and nitrogen. The remainder is tiny amounts of other gases.

LIFE ON EARTH

Living things need just the right amounts of **heat** and **light** from the **Sun**, as well as **food**, **water**, and **oxygen** to survive.

The Earth is the only planet in our **Solar System** known to support life, and it has taken millions and millions of years for conditions on our planet to become suitable for the plants and animals living here today.

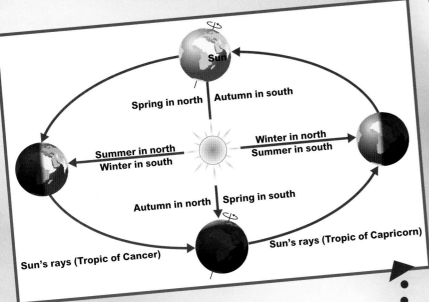

Sun

Spring in north | Autumn in south

Summer in north
Winter in south

Winter in north
Summer in south

Autumn in north | Spring in south

Sun's rays (Tropic of Cancer)

Sun's rays (Tropic of Capricorn)

The Earth going around the Sun.

Population

We use the word "**population**" to describe all the people living in a particular place. The world's population is greater today than ever before, and is increasing all the time.

Resources

This thriving population places ever greater demands on the Earth's **resources**, because of its need for **food**, **shelter**, and **fuel**. To accommodate these demands, people have changed the world around them to meet their needs.

- If all the land on Earth was shared equally among the entire population, we would all get an area equal in size to about 2.7 football pitches!

- The Earth is over 4 billion years old, but is only expected to support life for a further 500 million years.

- There are more than 1,000 artificial satellites and 21,000 pieces of man-made space debris currently orbiting the Earth!

- The length of a day on Earth is increasing by about 17 milliseconds per century!

Fun Facts

The force of gravity is not even all over the Earth. A person weighting 150 lbs at the equator would weight 151 lbs at the North Pole!

A green Earth makes a healthier environment.

Did You Know?

The part of Earth that has life on it is called the ecosphere.

ANCIENT LIFE

As we have learned, it has taken millions and millions of years for conditions on Earth to become suitable for the vast array of plant and animal species sharing the planet today. Scientists measure the Earth's history in **geological time**, which divides into four eras:

The Precambrian Supereon – 4,600 – 545 million years ago: The **first single-cell organisms** appeared during this time, and the **earliest known fossils** can be dated back to this era.

The Paleozoic Era – 545 - 250 million years ago: **Fossil records** suggest a huge increase in the number of different creatures living on Earth throughout this time, from **sea creatures** with **hard body coverings,** and small **arthropods** (creatures with jointed bodies), to the earliest **vertebrates** (animals with backbones) and **amphibians** (animals able to breathe in and out of water). At the end of this era, amphibians evolved into the earliest **reptiles**. They quickly spread throughout the land, which, at this time, was joined together in one vast **continent**.

The Mesozoic Era – 250 – 65 million years ago: The numbers of **reptiles** increased rapidly throughout this time, which also saw the appearance of the **dinosaurs**. They were the dominant vertebrate life forms until **65 million years ago**, when they suddenly died out, probably because of major changes to the Earth's **climate**.

Cenozoic Era – 65 million years ago – present day: The **age of mammals** began after the dinosaurs died out. It is thought that mammals may have survived the **climatic change** which wiped out the dinosaurs because they are able to **control their own body temperatures**.

Precambrian Supereon (Dawn of Life) – First single-celled organisms, and early many-celled, soft-bodied creatures.

Paleozoic Era (Ancient Life) – Many parts of the Earth became hot and humid, allowing plants, forests, and swamp creatures to thrive.

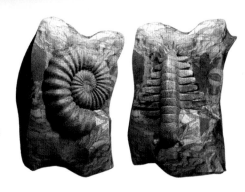

Cambrian Period – First creatures with hard outer shells.

Ordovician Period – First land plants and fish.

Silurian Period – First small land animals.

Devonian Period – First amphibians.

Carboniferous Period – Large insects; first reptiles and forests.

Permian Period – First swimming reptiles.

Mesozoic Era (Middle Life) – The Age of the Dinosaurs

Triassic Period – First dinosaurs and bony fish.

Jurassic Period – Large dinosaurs; first mammals and birds.

Cretaceous Period – First flowering plants.

Cenozoic Era (Recent Life) – The Age of Mammals

Tertiary Period – Modern mammals, invertebrates, and birds.

Quaternary Period – First humans.

Did You Know ?

The heaviest dinosaur, the Brachiosaurus, weighed 80 tonnes - that's about the same as 17 African Elephants!

PLANT LIFE ON EARTH

Plants!

Like all living things, plants rely on the gases in our **atmosphere** in order to survive, and it is thanks to them that we humans are able to breathe the air around us.

The very first **plant-like organisms** appeared in the Earth's oceans around 3,500 million years ago. They used light from the **Sun** to make food from **water** and **carbon dioxide**, releasing **oxygen** into the air as a by-product. This process is called **photosynthesis**, and was repeated over millions of years until there was enough oxygen in the atmosphere to support other forms of life.

Fun Facts

Some plants have evolved leaves, stings, or poisons to protect themselves from being eaten by animals!

Photosynthesis

The survival of almost all living things relies on the process of **photosynthesis**. Not only does it play an important role in maintaining the levels of **oxygen** and **carbon dioxide** in the **atmosphere**, it also keeps the plants we need for **food** healthy and ensures that they are able to **grow**, **reproduce**, and provide **habitats** - lush **rainforests** and shady **woodlands** - for a wide variety of **animal**, **bird**, and **insect** life.

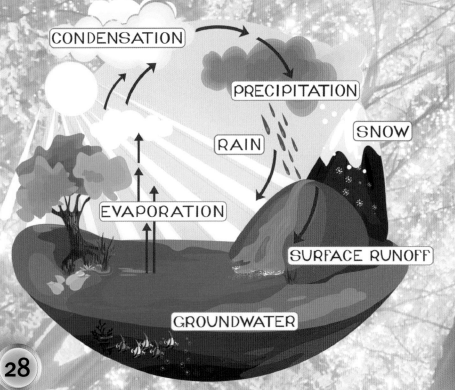

CONDENSATION

PRECIPITATION

SNOW

RAIN

EVAPORATION

SURFACE RUNOFF

GROUNDWATER

Adapting!

Like all living things, plants have had to adapt to their **environments** in order to survive. **Cacti** and many other **desert plants**, for example, store large quantities of water in their broad stems, and have **widespread root systems** that are able to collect water from a distance, because they grow in dry areas where there is very little rainfall.

- Everything we eat comes from plants, either directly, when we eat the plants ourselves, or indirectly, when the animals we eat feed on plants.

- All plants can be divided into two groups: **flowering plants**, including **roses, sunflowers**, and most types of **tree**, and **non-flowering plants**, such as **mosses** and **ferns**.

- Some plants eat insects, and other very tiny animals. They are called **carnivorous plants**, and grow in areas where the soil is thin, and lacking in nutrients.

Climates!

Arctic poppies, on the other hand, grow well in **cold climates**, on **mountains** and in **dry river beds**. They thrive amongst stones which absorb heat from the Sun, and provide shelter for their roots. Their flowers continually turn to face the Sun, tracking its progress across the sky.

Did You Know?

There are around 300,000 plant species living in the world today.

WATER WATER EVERYWHERE!

Around **71%** of the **Earth's surface is covered in water,** which makes up five huge **oceans**, and many smaller **seas**.

The world's oceans are not only very important to life on Earth, providing homes for vast numbers of living things, but also influence the **weather,** and **climate conditions** across the globe.

Ocean water is constantly moving in huge bands called **currents**.

The water absorbs **heat** from the **Sun**, particularly in **tropical regions**, and carries it all over the Earth in **surface currents**, which affect the top 350 metres of the ocean.

Fun Facts

Around 70% of the oxygen we breath is produced by the oceans!
The name 'Pacific Ocean' comes from the Latin "Tepre Pacificum" meaning "Peaceful Sea"

Very cold water from the **North and South Poles** sinks beneath the warmer surface currents and drifts towards the equator, where it is warmed by the Sun, and becomes a **surface current** itself. It then changes direction, drifting back towards the Poles, where it becomes a colder, **deep current** again.

Seas and oceans are constantly moved by **tides**, which are caused by the **Moon**.

As the Moon travels around the Earth, the force of its **gravity** makes the water on either side of the Earth bulge. In a 24 hour period, this causes two **high tides**, and two **low tides**, when sea levels are at their highest and lowest respectively.

Lake Superior is the largest of the Great Lakes of North America.

Did You Know ?

The Pacific is the largest of the world's oceans, and covers around 30% of the Earth's surface!

Rivers

Rivers form where **streams** join together, flowing across the land and eventually into a **sea** or **lake**.

Rivers alter the surface of the Earth over time by **eroding** the **rocks** they flow over, and by depositing **rocks, pebbles, sand,** and **silt** as they go.

At 6,853 km (4,258 miles) long, The Nile is the world's longest river!

SEA CREATURES!

The Earth's oceans are home to a startling array of plants and animals that live and feed at different levels of the water.

These levels are called **zones**.

The **sunlit zone** is home to all **ocean plants** and many animals from **corals** and **jellyfish**, to **seals, sea turtles**, and **sharks**. Billions of **microscopic plants** called **phytoplankton** drift near the surface of the water, and provide food for many of the creatures living within the ocean's depths.

Only a little light filters down to the **twilight zone**, so the animals that live here have adapted to life in near darkness, and are able to survive in very cold temperatures. These include **octopuses**, **squid**, **crabs**, and **lobsters**.

Fun Facts

A female octopus is called a "hen"! The Giant Pacific Octopus lays clutches of around 100,000 eggs!

The **sunless zone** is extremely cold, and the animals that live here feed mainly on dead **plankton**, which sinks from the surface of the water. This zone is extremely deep - it is difficult for humans to explore because the pressure of the water is so high. Animals that live here include **lantern fish, cookiecutter sharks**, and **deep sea jellyfish**.

The **abyssal zone** is freezing cold and completely dark. Many of the animals that live here, such as the **anglerfish** can produce light from their bodies to attract prey.

Did You Know ?

Most of an octopus's body is spongy and flexible, but its eyes are more solid. Most species of octopus can squeeze through tight spaces that are only slightly larger than their eyes! Bizarrely, an octopus's eyes remain at the same orientation regardless of its position, so if it turns on its side, or even flips upside down, its gaze will remain fixed!

- There are a million known species of plant and animal living in the world's oceans, and many more have yet to be discovered.

- Around 65,000 newly "discovered" species are still waiting to be given formal names.

- Coral reefs cover less than 1% of the ocean floor, but support around 25% of all marine creatures.

WEATHER CONDITIONS

What is Weather?

We use the word "**weather**" to describe the conditions in the **atmosphere** close to the Earth's surface. These conditions include **air temperature, wind speed, air pressure,** and the amount of water in the air, which we call **humidity**. Other factors include how **cloudy** it is, and whether there is any **precipitation (rain** or **snow)**.

The **Sun** plays a crucial part in determining the weather. Its rays have the strongest effect where they hit the surface of the Earth directly, around the planet's centre, or **equator**. The further away from the equator you are, the more the heat is spread over a larger area, so the weather is cooler.

Fun Facts

Regions along the equator receive the same strength of sunlight all year round. These places have only two distinguishable seasons: wet, and dry.

Different seasons

Weather conditions change throughout the year because the Earth is tilted on its **axis**. As the Earth **orbits** the Sun, the Sun's rays fall on different areas, causing the **seasons.**

The four major seasons are spring, summer, autumn, and winter.

Look how these trees respond to changes in the seasons.

Now it's sunny, now it's not...

Heat from the Sun causes water from the seas to **evaporate.** As the **water vapour** rises and cools, it **condenses**, forming tiny **water droplets** which group together to form **clouds**.

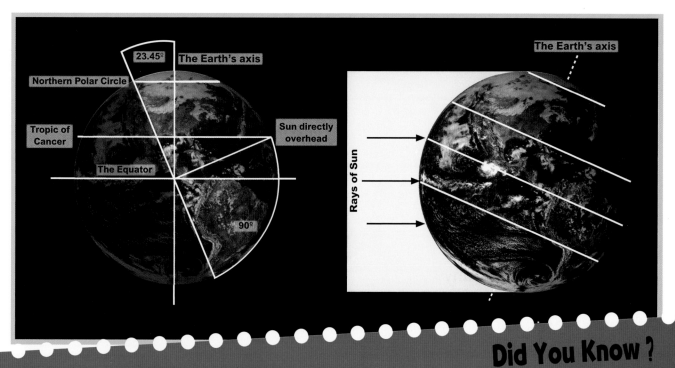

23.45°

The Earth's axis

Northern Polar Circle

Tropic of Cancer

Sun directly overhead

The Equator

90°

The Earth's axis

Rays of Sun

Did You Know ?

When the North Pole of the Earth is tilted towards the Sun, we in the northern hemisphere get more sunlight: this is our summer. As the Earth travels around the Sun, the tilt of the North Pole changes. When it is tilted away from the Sun we receive less sunlight and it is winter. In between we have autumn and spring.

THE EARTH'S CLIMATE

Typical weather conditions and patterns in a region over time are known as its **climate**. Climates depend on the position of an area on the Earth's surface, and, accordingly, how much sunlight can reach it, as well as its **distance from the sea**, and its **height above sea level**.

Mountain climates drop as the **altitude** (height above sea level) increases, affecting the types of **vegetation** that are able to grow.

Polar climates are extremely cold and change very little throughout the year. There is hardly any rain or snowfall, and very few plants can grow. Polar animals have thick layers of fur or fat to keep them warm.

A snow leopard is perfectly suited to the cold environment.

Desert climates are very dry, and there is hardly any rainfall. Daytime temperatures are extremely warm, but can plummet over night. Many plants and animals that live in the desert can store water.

Mediterranean regions are warm all year round, but tend to be wet in **winter** and dry in **summer**. **Citrus fruits** grow well in Mediterranean climates because their thick skins prevent them from drying out in hot weather.

Areas around the **equator** are known as **equatorial regions**, and are permanently hot and wet; ideal conditions for **rainforests**.

City climates are usually warmer than the less built-up areas around them because concrete absorbs and retains heat for longer than vegetation.

In **temperate regions** the weather is changeable. Rain falls throughout the year, and temperatures vary according to the **season**.

Coastal or **maritime climates** are **mild** and **wet** because the air above the land and sea is constantly circulating, gaining and losing heat throughout the day and night.

The magnificent sea turtle.

Fun Facts

Tundra regions are known for their harsh winds and low winter temperatures. Only hardy, low-growing plants such a **lichens** are able to survive here.

Did You Know ?

Tropical climates are warm all year round. There are only two seasons: the dry season, and the wet season.

HABITATS

Tigers have **striped fur** to help them hide amongst the long grasses and blend in with the sunlight filtering through the treetops to the jungle floor. With their **stealthy hunting methods**, huge paws, **sharp claws** and **fearsome** jaws, tigers are **formidable predators** and are well adapted to thrive in the **grasslands** and **forests** in which they live.

Frogs are highly adapted animals.

The tiger is the biggest cat in the world.

Tree frogs eat insects and other small animals. Many can **change colour** to blend in with their surroundings and surprise their prey. They have **sticky pads** on their feet to stop them falling.

Fun Facts

In order to thrive in their natural surroundings, plants and animals have had to adapt to the world around them.

38

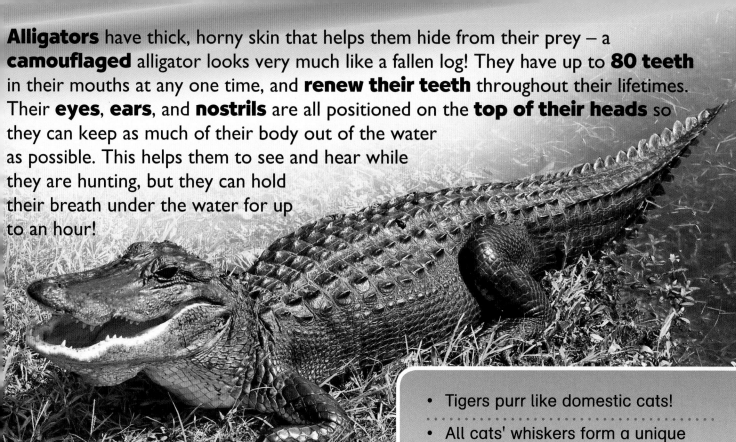

Alligators have thick, horny skin that helps them hide from their prey – a **camouflaged** alligator looks very much like a fallen log! They have up to **80 teeth** in their mouths at any one time, and **renew their teeth** throughout their lifetimes. Their **eyes**, **ears**, and **nostrils** are all positioned on the **top of their heads** so they can keep as much of their body out of the water as possible. This helps them to see and hear while they are hunting, but they can hold their breath under the water for up to an hour!

Did You Know ?

The word 'animal' comes from the Latin word 'anima', which means breathing.

- Tigers purr like domestic cats!
- All cats' whiskers form a unique pattern, rather like our fingerprints.
- The tortoise is one of the oldest animals on Earth, dating back to 250 million years, before the dinosaurs. In Japan people gave them as wedding gifts to wish the bride and groom a long and happy life!

Dolphins and **whales** are **marine mammals**, which means that, unlike fish, they **breathe air** and give birth to **live young**. Dolphins have **excellent eyesight** and **hearing**, and can **communicate** with each other by making **clicking** and **whistling sounds**. They make particularly **high-pitched clicking sounds** to help them **navigate** and find food. This process is known as **echolocation.**

OPEN TO CHANGE

In order to thrive in their natural surroundings, plants and animals have had to **adapt** to the world around them.

Kangaroos, for example, are ideally suited to life in the **harsh climate** of the **Australian outback** because they are able to survive for long periods without water. When they do need to look for food and water, they can reach speeds of up to **70 kilometres an hour**, and their **energy-efficient** way of travelling mean that they can cover long distances in no time!

Fun Facts

The red kangaroo is the world's largest marsupial. Females have one baby at a time, which at birth is smaller than a cherry!.

Tropical pitchers are carnivorous plants that lure prey into their traps with their **sweet smell** and **sugary nectar**. As well as unsuspecting insects, larger species of pitcher plant are able to attract and digest larger animals, including mice and lizards.

Most species are found in **southeast Asia**. It is believed that monkeys drink rainwater out of the pitcher-shaped plants, giving them their alternative name: **"monkey cups"**!

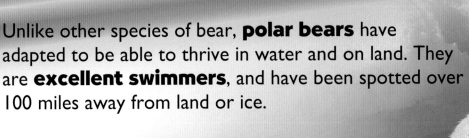

Unlike other species of bear, **polar bears** have adapted to be able to thrive in water and on land. They are **excellent swimmers**, and have been spotted over 100 miles away from land or ice.

They have large, **furry-soled feet** which not only help them to spread their weight on snow and ice, but also keep them warm and stop them slipping. As well as providing **insulation**, their **white fur** provides a **camouflage**, and their **small ears prevent heat loss** in the freezing Arctic climate.

They may not be pretty, but vultures are nature's cleaning agents!

Polar bears are found in the Arctic, the lands around the North Pole, where it is near impossible for human beings to survive.

Vultures are scavengers. They glide on air currents, searching the ground below for carcasses to feed upon. Their bald heads and necks help them to stay clean by preventing bacteria from animal remains from festering in their feathers and spreading disease.

Did You Know ?

Polar bears actually have black skins and colourless fur! Their thick, hollow hairs reflect light, giving the bears their white-looking coats.

NATURAL RESOURCES

As we have already learned, the world's growing **population** is placing ever greater demands on the planet's **resources**. Many of these resources are beneath the Earth's surface. These include **precious stones**, **metals**, and **fuels.**

Fossil Fuels

Coal, **oil**, and **gas** are known as **fossil fuels**. They have many uses, including running motor vehicles and generating **electricity**.

Fossil fuels are formed from the remains of plants and animals that have been buried in rock for millions of years. The **chemical energy** trapped in these **organisms** is released as they are burned.

Because demand for these fuels is so great, and they take such a long time to form, supplies are limited.

Nuclear Power

Radioactive substances produce **nuclear energy** when their **atoms** are broken apart. Many people believe that **nuclear power** could be the most efficient, and convenient, energy source of the future, but it creates hazardous **radioactive waste**, which is difficult to dispose of safely.

Mining

Mining and **extracting fuels** and **ores** from beneath the surface of the Earth is a difficult – and expensive – process, made harder by the fact that many sources have already been used up.

Re-using and **recycling** materials help to make the Earth's **natural resources** last longer, but scientists are having to look for other sources of fuel to meet the population's growing needs.

Coal, one of nature's most valuable natural resources, is created from dead plant matter!

Renewable Energy!

Only 5% of the Earth's energy comes from **renewable sources**, that is, sources of energy that will not run out. These include heat from the Sun (**solar energy**), and from underground rocks (**geothermal energy**), as well as wind, which can be used to turn **wind turbines**, and moving water, which is used in **hydroelectric power stations**.

Renewable energy is often less reliable and efficient than fossil fuels because it relies on certain weather conditions in order to be effective.

Fun Facts

The largest wind turbines generate enough electricity to supply around 600 homes!

Did You Know?

Coal has the largest remaining reserves of all the fossil fuels, but as the growing population continues to use more and more, demand is soon likely to outstrip supply. It is thought that we currently have enough coal to meet around 180 years of global production.

GLOSSARY

Amphibian: A type of cold-blooded, soft-skinned animal that can live on land and in water.

Atmosphere: 1) The protective layer of gases around the Earth that enables plants and animals to survive. 2) A layer of gases surrounding any planet.

Big Bang theory: The idea that the Universe came into being because of a massive explosion called the Big Bang.

Climate: The typical weather patterns in an area over a sustained period of time.

Continents: The landmasses into which the Earth's crust is divided.

Desert: A climate that is very dry, with less than 250mm of rainfall a year.

Earthquake: A sudden movement of rock in the Earth's crust which releases built up pressure.

Epicentre: The point on the Earth's surface directly above the focus of an earthquake.

Equator: An imaginary line running around the centre of the Earth, dividing it into the northern and southern hemispheres.

Faults: Cracks in the Earth's surface, caused by the movements of plates.

Geological Time: A scale of millions of years used by geologists to measure different phases of the Earth's history.

Geologist: A scientist concerned with the study of the Earth's origin and structure.

Global Warming: A rise in global temperatures believed to be the result of the Greenhouse Effect

Greenhouse Effect: The trapping of heat within the Earth's atmosphere.

Hot Spot: An area on the Earth's surface burned by particularly hot currents of magma.

Jgneous Rock: Rock formed when magma (molten rock) cools and becomes solid.

Lava: Magma that has erupted onto the surface of the Earth.

Magma: Molten, underground rock which forms part of the Earth's mantle.

Metamorphic Rock: The type of rock formed when another rock is changed by intense heat or pressure or both.

Nuclear Energy: Energy held within the nucleus of tiny particles called atoms.

Orbit: The path of a circling object.

Pangaea: A single giant landmass that began to divide around 225 million years ago, leading to formation of the continents we know today.

Renewable Energy: Sources of energy that will not run out.

Sedimentary Rock: Rock formed when mineral particles are deposited, buried, and squashed into layers.

Seismic Waves: Waves that spread outwards from the centre of an earthquake.

Volcano: An opening in the Earth's surface formed by magma bursting out in an explosion.